Julie Brc

Introduction

This book contains 50 of the most delicious recipes you will find for pancakes. It has recipes for sweet pancakes and also lots of savory recipes. I am a great fan of eating pancakes not just for breakfast but for later in day as well!

Along with a really wide selection I have made sure to use the most common household ingredients and measurements so all of these recipes are easy to cook. If you have kids, then making pancakes can be a great way to get them involved in the kitchen as well as having a lot of fun along the way.

Try to ensure you follow the recipes here pretty closely in terms of the measurements. Use a wooden spoon to do the mixing – just ensure you don't go overboard here. Mixing the batter until everything is just combined is the best way to go to avoid overly chewy pancakes.

Try to get hold of a griddle or a nice, heavy pan to use to stop the bottom getting burned and sticking. To eliminate any burning still further give the bottom of the pan or griddle a quick spray of cooking oil spray. You will know when to turn over the pancake as soon as you see the bubbles on one side come up.

Flip them over straightaway once they appear. You don't have to cook them long at all – a couple of minutes on either side will be plenty. Once they are lovely and golden brown they are done. You will very quickly come to recognise the look and smell of a perfectly cooked pancake!

Serve your pancakes hot, straight from the griddle or keep them warm for a few minutes while you cook the whole batch to enjoy together.

I've cooked all of these both as a professional chef and as mom at home and I really hope you will love eating these pancakes as much as my family has done so over the past 20 years.

Julie

Contents

Almond flour pancake

Ingredients

1 cup almond flour
1/3 cup coconut milk
2 eggs
2 tablespoons maple syrup
Sea salt, to taste
Coconut oil, for cooking

Directions

In a large mixing bowl, combine all of the ingredients, except the coconut oil, and mix together well with a wooden spoon. Over medium heat, heat the coconut oil in a large skillet. Add nearly ¼ cup of batter onto the skillet, cooking until bubbles appear. When you see the bubbles forming, flip the pancakes and cook until golden brown. Top with fresh berries, nuts, butter, whipped coconut cream, a little cinnamon, stevia, raw honey, some maple syrup or any of your other favorite toppings.

Apple and cinnamon pancakes

For the pancakes
¾ cup milk
1½ tablespoons vinegar
1 cup flour
3 tablespoons sugar
1 teaspoon cinnamon
1 teaspoon baking powder
½ teaspoon baking soda
½ teaspoon salt
1 egg
2 tablespoons oil
For the apple sauce
2 tablespoon butter
2 apples, peeled, cored, and diced
2 tablespoons brown sugar
½ teaspoon cinnamon
⅓ cup of maple syrup

Directions

Heat a skillet to medium-high heat. Whisk together the milk and vinegar and allow to rest for 5 minutes. In a large bowl, whisk together flour, sugar, baking powder, baking soda, and salt. In another bowl, whisk the egg and oil into milk. Add wet ingredients to dry ingredients and stir until combined. Pour ¼ cup of batter onto the skillet. Cook until bubbles form. Flip the pancake and until golden brown. Set pancakes aside and repeat with remaining batter. Add butter, apples, brown sugar, and cinnamon to a medium sauce pan. Stir over medium heat until apples are tender. Add in the syrup. Serve apple topping over warm pancakes.

Apple ring pancakes

Ingredients

2 Large Apples - Granny Smith is perfect
1 Cup Flour
¼ cup brown sugar
1 teaspoon baking powder
¼ teaspoon nutmeg
1 teaspoon cinnamon
¼ teaspoon salt
¼ cup reduced fat (or fat free) sour cream
1 egg
1 teaspoon vanilla extract
¾ cup sparkling water or club soda

Directions

Preheat a griddle or skillet to medium heat. Coat lightly with cooking spray. Peel and core the apples. Cut the apples into roughly ¼ inch slices. In a large bowl, combine the flour, brown sugar, baking powder, nutmeg, cinnamon and salt until well mixed. In a separate bowl, add the sour cream, egg and vanilla and mix until combined. Make a well in the dry ingredients, add the wet ingredients and stir until just combined. Add the sparkling water and stir. One at a time, dip the apple slices into the batter and place on the hot griddle. Allow the pancakes to cook until the edges start to look dry and then flip over. Cooking the other side until golden brown. Repeat for all apple slices and serve.

Bacon pancakes

Ingredients

1 cup all-purpose flour
½ cup whole wheat pastry flour
2 tablespoons sugar
2 teaspoons baking powder
¼ teaspoon baking soda
1 teaspoon salt
1 cup buttermilk
2 eggs
4 tablespoons unsalted butter, melted
1 teaspoon vanilla
4-5 strips smoked bacon, cooked and crumbled
2 bananas, thinly sliced
Butter for griddle

Directions

In a large bowl, whisk together flours, sugar, baking powder, baking soda, and salt. In a separate bowl or large measuring cup, whisk together buttermilk, eggs, butter, and vanilla. Pour wet ingredients into dry ingredients and mix until just combined. Heat a griddle over medium-high heat. Pour batter onto griddle. Top with slices of banana and crumbled bacon. Cook until bubbles form on top of pancakes, then flip and cook until golden on the underside. Serve pancakes warm with butter and maple syrup and extra banana slices and bacon.

Banana, Nutella and oatmeal pancakes

Ingredients

1 cup all-purpose flour
¼ cup quick oats
1 teaspoon baking soda
¼ teaspoon kosher salt
2 tablespoons granulated sugar
1 large banana, mashed
1 cup buttermilk
1 tablespoon extra virgin coconut oil
1 large egg
½ teaspoon pure vanilla extract
¼ cup Nutella

Directions

In a large mixing bowl add the flour, oats, baking soda, salt, sugar, banana, buttermilk, coconut oil, egg and vanilla, stirring until well combined. Gently stir in Nutella but don't fully mix in. Spoon batter on to the griddle over medium heat. Let it cook until bubbles appear. Flip and cook until golden brown. Transfer to a plate to eat straightaway or keep warm while you continue to cook the remaining pancakes. Serve pancakes with maple syrup and whichever chopped fruit you like.

Basic pancake recipe

Ingredients

1 ½ cups all-purpose flour
3 ½ teaspoons baking powder
1 teaspoon salt
1 tablespoon white sugar
1 ¼ cups milk
1 egg
3 tablespoons butter

Directions

Grab a large bowl and whisk together the flour, baking powder, salt and sugar. Make a well in the middle of the bowl and gradually pour in the milk, egg and melted butter. Now mix everything together until all the lumps disappear. Heat the griddle or pan up over a medium heat. Take about ¼ cup of the batter and pour it onto the griddle. Once bubbles start to appear, flip over the pancake and cook until golden brown. Serve hot straight from the griddle!

Beer pancakes

Ingredients

2 cups all-purpose flour
2 tablespoons sugar
4 teaspoons baking powder
1 teaspoon salt
12-ounce can of beer
1/4 cup canola oil

Directions

Place dry ingredients in a medium-size bowl and mix in beer and oil. Heat a lightly greased skillet over medium heat. To make one pancake, spoon three tablespoons of batter onto skillet; cook two to three minutes per side until browned. You can substitute root beer for a non-alcoholic breakfast.

Blueberry and buttermilk pancakes

Ingredients

2 cups all-purpose flour
3 tablespoons granulated sugar
1 teaspoon baking powder
¾ teaspoon fine salt
½ teaspoon baking soda
2 cups buttermilk
2 large eggs
4 tablespoons melted, unsalted butter
Vegetable oil
2 cups fresh or frozen blueberries
Maple syrup, for serving

Directions

Heat the oven to 200°F and place a rack in the middle. Put a baking sheet on the rack. Add the flour, sugar, baking powder, salt, and baking soda into a large bowl and whisk until evenly combined. Place the buttermilk, eggs, and melted butter in a medium bowl and whisk until evenly combined. Add the buttermilk mixture to the flour mixture and stir until the flour is just incorporated. Let it rest for 5 minutes. Heat a large frying pan, skillet or griddle over medium heat for about 4 minutes.

When the pan is ready put about ¼ of a cup of the batter onto the pan for each pancake. Evenly sprinkle each pancake with 1/4 cup of the blueberries. Cook until bubbles appear and then flip over. Cook until golden brown. Transfer the pancakes to a plate to eat straightaway or keep in the oven to remain warm. Repeat with the remaining batter. Serve with maple syrup.

Blueberry pancakes

Ingredients

1 3/4 cups all-purpose flour
2 tablespoons sugar
1 teaspoon baking powder
1/2 teaspoon baking soda
1/2 teaspoon salt
2 large eggs
1 cup milk, plus more if needed
1 cup sour cream
1 stick butter, melted
1/2 teaspoon vanilla extract
1 1/2 cups fresh or frozen blueberries
1/2 teaspoon lemon zest

Directions

Sift the flour, sugar, baking powder, baking soda and salt into a large mixing bowl. In a separate large bowl, lightly whisk the eggs. Add the milk, sour cream, half the melted butter and the vanilla, whisking to blend. Gradually pour the egg mixture into the dry ingredients and everything together until blended. Slowly fold the blueberries and lemon zest into the batter. Heat a large skillet or griddle over medium heat and cover with some of the remaining melted butter. Place about 1/4 of a cup on the griddle for each pancake. When bubbles begin to form on the pancake and the outer edge looks done, flip it over and cook briefly until golden brown on the other side.

Canadian pancakes

Ingredients

3 eggs
125g plain flour
1 tablespoon baking powder
25g castor sugar
235 ml milk

Directions

Separate the whites from the yolks of the eggs. Whisk the egg whites until stiff. Sieve the flour and baking powder into a bowl and add to this the sugar, yolks and milk. Whisk together until smooth. Fold the egg whites into the batter. Lightly oil a pan or skillet and place over a medium heat. Pour a ¼ of a cup of batter into the pan and cook until golden brown on both sides. Remove the pancakes from the heat to a plate to eat now or keep warm in the oven. Continue cooking the rest of the batter. Serve with maple syrup.

Cheesy pancakes

Ingredients

2 cups flour
2 eggs
2 teaspoons baking powder
2 ½ cups milk
½ cup oil or melted butter
½ teaspoon salt
1 teaspoon vinegar
Grated cheese
Syrup

Directions

Sift all the dry ingredients together. Add the liquids gradually. Mix all together. Put some batter into a greased pan and spread evenly. Sprinkle a generous handful of cheese evenly over the pancake. Flip it over when golden brown to allow the cheese to melt into the pancake. The longer you leave it the crispier it will become. When you are happy with the pancake simply put it on a plate, fold it over and enjoy.

Chickpea pancakes

Ingredients

1 cup chickpea flour
1 teaspoon salt
1 teaspoon freshly ground black pepper
4 to 6 tablespoons olive oil
½ large onion, thinly sliced
2 teaspoons chopped fresh rosemary

Directions

Heat the oven to about 430. Put a 12-inch pizza pan or cast-iron skillet in oven. Put the chickpea flour in a bowl and add the salt and pepper. Slowly add 1 cup lukewarm water, whisking to eliminate lumps. Stir in 2 tablespoons olive oil. Cover and let sit for 15 minutes. The batter should be about the consistency of heavy cream.

Remove the pan and pour 2 tablespoons of the oil into it and swirl around. Add the onions, return the pan to the oven and cook, stirring once or twice, until they're well browned. Stir the onions and rosemary into the batter, then immediately pour the batter into the pan. Bake for 10 to 15 minutes, or until the pancake is firm and the edges set. Heat the broiler and brush the top of the pancake with 1 or 2 tablespoons of oil. Put the pancake a few inches away from the broiler and cook just long enough to brown it in spots. Cut it into wedges, and serve hot.

Chocolate Chip pancakes

Ingredients

3 cups flour
6 tablespoons sugar
¼ teaspoon salt
2 tablespoons baking powder
3 eggs
⅓ cup canola oil
1 cup milk
Chocolate chips

Instructions

Mix the dry ingredients. In a separate bowl mix the wet ingredients. Combine wet and dry ingredients. Add milk if needed to get the right consistency. Put ¼ cup of the batter over medium heat or a griddle and sprinkle on the chocolate chips. Turn over when the bubbles appear and cook the other side. Serve hot.

Coconut flour pancakes

Ingredients

4 Eggs
¼ cup Milk
3 tablespoons of oil
¼ cup organic coconut flour
1 tablespoon sugar
¼ teaspoon sea salt
¼ teaspoon baking powder

Directions

Preheat a griddle to medium heat. Whisk together the eggs, oil and milk in a large bowl until well combined. In a different bowl sift the coconut flour, sugar, salt and baking powder. Add the contents of the two bowls together and thoroughly mix until there are no lumps. Put about ¼ cup of the batter onto the preheated griddle and cook until the bubbles begin to appear. Flip over straightaway and cook until golden brown on the other side. Serve hot.

Coffee pancakes

Ingredients

1 cup whole wheat pastry flour or white wheat flour
2 tablespoons sugar
1 teaspoon baking powder
1 teaspoon baking soda
¼ teaspoon salt
1 cup low-fat buttermilk
1 large egg
2 tablespoons instant coffee granules
1 tablespoon unsalted butter, melted and cooled

Directions

In a large bowl, whisk together the flour, sugar, baking powder, baking soda and salt. Set the bowl aside. In a medium bowl, whisk to combine the buttermilk, egg, instant coffee, and cooled, melted butter. Using a spatula, add the wet ingredients to the dry and mix to combine. Preheat griddle or large, non-stick skillet over medium heat. Once hot, put about ¼ cup batter onto the hot surface and spread to a 4-inch diameter. When bubbles appear flip the pancake and cook an additional 1-2 minutes. Repeat with the rest of the batter and serve hot.

Cranberry pancakes

Ingredients

½ cup fresh cranberries
¼ cup all-purpose flour
2 teaspoons whole-wheat flour
1 tablespoon yellow cornmeal
1 tablespoon sugar
½ teaspoon baking powder
1/8 teaspoon salt
1/8 teaspoon ground nutmeg, or ¼ teaspoon vanilla extract
6 tablespoons non-fat milk
2 tablespoons pasteurized egg substitute, such as Egg Beaters
1 ½ teaspoons walnut or canola oil

Directions

Boil 2 inches of water in a small saucepan. Add the cranberries and boil for another 2 minutes. Drain and cool for 5 minutes. Meanwhile, whisk all-purpose flour, whole-wheat flour, cornmeal, sugar, baking powder, salt and nutmeg (if using) in a large bowl. In another, smaller bowl whisk milk, egg substitute, oil and vanilla (if using). Coarsely chop the cranberries and stir into the milk mixture. Now stir the milk mixture into the dry ingredients until combined. Coat a griddle or large non-stick skillet with cooking spray and heat over medium heat. Using ¼ cup of batter for each pancake, cook 2 pancakes at a time until bubbles appear. Flip and continue cooking until golden brown. Repeat with the remaining batter.

Crepes

Ingredients

100g plain flour
2 large eggs
300ml milk
1 tablespoon sunflower or vegetable oil, plus a little extra for frying
Lemon juice
Caster sugar

Directions

Place the flour, eggs, milk and a pinch of salt into a bowl or large jug, then whisk into a smooth batter. Leave the mixture to rest for 30 mins (if you have time). Set a frying pan over a medium heat and carefully wipe it with some oiled kitchen paper. When hot, poor some batter into the centre of the pan and carefully tilt the pan so that the mixture covers the whole surface. Cook for 1 min on each side until golden brown. Keep your cooked pancakes warm in the oven while you finish the batter. Sprinkle with lemon and sugar and serve hot.

Delicate pear pancakes

Ingredients

4 large pears, thickly chopped.
2 heaped tablespoons light muscovado (brown) sugar
50g butter (unsalted)
Optional
300ml crème fresh
300ml fromage frais

Directions

Have 6 pancakes ready-made. If they are not already warm, warm them in an oven at 150C. Heat the butter in a large frying pan and let is dissolve, covering the whole pan. Add the pears. Fry for 2-3 minutes on a high heat, until the undersides are golden. Turn the pears over and sprinkle with sugar. Cook for a further 2-3 minutes until the sugar dissolves and the pan juice becomes sticky. Add the pears to the pancakes and serve. They can be served on their own or with crème fresh or fromage frais.

Dutch baby pancakes

Ingredients

3 tablespoons butter
2 eggs room temperature
1 egg white, room temperature
2/3 cup whole milk at room temperature
2 tablespoons granulated sugar
1/2 cup plus 2 tablespoons flour
1/2 teaspoon vanilla extract
1/4 teaspoon ground cinnamon
A pinch of nutmeg
1/4 teaspoon kosher salt
Powdered sugar, cinnamon, and lemon juice for topping as desired

Directions

Preheat the oven to 400F. Place the 10" cast iron skillet in the oven and heat for at least 8 minutes. Melt 3 tablespoons butter in a saucepan or in the microwave. In a blender, put the eggs, egg white, milk, 1 tablespoon melted butter, sugar, flour, vanilla, nutmeg, cinnamon, and salt. Blend until the batter is smooth and creamy. Remove the hot skillet from the oven. Pour the remaining 2 tablespoons melted butter into the pan and swirl to coat the bottom.

Gently pour the batter into the hot skillet. Return the pan to the oven and bake for 20 minutes. Once the Dutch baby is done baking, remove the skillet from the oven and use a thin spatula to gently guide the pancake onto a large plate. Cut into wedges and sprinkle with cinnamon, powdered sugar, and a dash of lemon juice.

Egg nog pancakes

Ingredients

2 cups white whole wheat flour
4 ½ teaspoons baking powder
½ tsp salt
1 ½ teaspoons cinnamon
2 teaspoons sugar
1 teaspoons nutmeg
2 large eggs
2 cups Silk Nog
2 tablespoons water
2 teaspoons vanilla
Cooking spray

Directions

Mix all dry ingredients in a bowl. Add the wet ingredients to the mixing bowl and mix well with a spoon Heat a large skillet on medium heat. Lightly spray oil to coat and pour ¼ cup of pancake batter. When the bubbles settle and the edges begin to set, flip the pancakes. Repeat with the remainder of the batter and serve.

Four ingredient protein pancakes

Ingredients

1 large banana, mashed
2 eggs
1/8 teaspoon baking powder
2 tablespoons vanilla whey protein powder or a little vanilla extract

Directions

Place a medium skillet over medium heat on the stove and let it heat up. Mash the banana with a fork. Add the eggs, baking powder, and protein powder or vanilla extract. Whisk until it is well combined. Spray the skillet with non-stick cooking spray before adding in 2-3 tablespoons of the pancake mixture. Let the pancakes cook until bubbles appear. Flip the pancake over and cook for other side until golden brown. When done place on a plate and serve with butter or fruit or sugar-free syrup.

French Pancakes

Ingredients

75g flour
1 egg
200ml milk
50g sugar
25g melted butter
Some vanilla

Directions

Whisk together all ingredients (I prefer to start with the dry ingredients and the egg, butter and half of the milk, this allows me to get rid of clumps, after that I add the rest of the milk). Leave to stand for up to one hour. Heat a frying pan and distribute the batter on the pan, using the complete surface and keeping it very thin. Crepes have to be thin, there is no raising agent to lighten up the pancake, so making it thick will likely make it very heavy.

Greek yogurt pancakes

Ingredients

1½ cups all-purpose flour
2 teaspoons of baking powder
2 tablespoons sugar (this is an optional extra!)
½ teaspoon salt
2 tablespoons oil
2 eggs
1 teaspoon vanilla (or ½ teaspoon almond extract)
¾ cup plain Greek yogurt (or vanilla Greek yogurt)
¾ cup milk (fat free is fine)
Topping ideas: yogurt, syrup, honey, fruit

Directions

Preheat a pan or griddle. Whisk together the flour, baking powder, sugar, and salt. Put this bowl aside. In another bowl, Mix the oil, eggs, vanilla and Greek yogurt into a different bowl. Add the two bowls together and stir. Stir in milk until all ingredients are combined. Grease griddle and pour ¼ - ⅓ cup batter onto the griddle. Allow to cook until bubbles form in the batter. Use a spatula to flip the pancake over and allow to cook for roughly another minute or until golden brown. Transfer to a platter and repeat until you have used all of the batter. Top pancakes with your favourite toppings such as more yogurt, syrup, honey, and fruit.

Hazelnut pancakes

Ingredients

1 cup ground hazelnuts
2 large eggs
2 tablespoons oil
1 tablespoons sweetener (recipe is calculated using sugar)
1/3 cup water

Directions

Combine all ingredients in a bowl. If the mixture seems too thick, add additional water. Cook on a griddle as you would any other pancakes (except the tops may not bubble - lift the pancake to check for doneness - they should be golden brown). You may need to spread these out a little thinner with your spatula if you like thinner pancakes. Serve hot.

Leek and mushroom pancakes

Ingredients

1 leek-sliced
2 large flat field mushrooms- chopped
Olive oil for frying
1/2-1 teaspoon wholegrain mustard
1 dessertspoon butter
1 dessert spoon plain flour
Cup of milk
Mixed peppercorns
Parmesan cheese, grated
Pancake batter

Directions

Prepare the pancake batter and put aside. In a saucepan fry the leek until soft then add mushroom and fry till cooked. Add the butter and when it's all melted add the flour and cook for a couple of minutes stirring continuously. Take off the heat and add half of the milk a little at a time. Add the mustard and return to the heat. Bring to the boil stirring continuously and add more milk as required to get the right consistency. Grind plenty of peppercorns into the mix and leave on a low heat. Make a plate sized pancake. Put it on a plate. Spoon the filling on to one half, sprinkle parmesan on top and fold the pancake over.

Lemon and raisin pancakes

Ingredients

Grated zest of half a lemon
100g self-rising flour
25g golden caster sugar
1 egg
125ml milk
50g raisins or sultanas

Directions

Mix the lemon zest, flour and sugar in a bowl. Stir in the egg and milk until well combined and pour the batter into a jug. Preheat a pan or a griddle and grease lightly with oil or butter. Pour batter until it spreads about 2 inches across. Sprinkle a few raisins onto the batter. When the pancakes begin to bubble up on the first side, flip them over and cook on the other side for another minute or so. Remove to a plate either to eat straightaway or keep warm in the oven. Serve hot!

Mac and cheese pancakes

Ingredients

60g self-rising flour
175g milk
1 egg
Pinch of salt
200g macaroni
200g grated Cheddar
1 teaspoon mustard
Oil or butter, to fry
Any cheese

Directions

Cook your pasta and let it cool. Add the flour to a bowl and add the salt. In a separate bowl whisk together the milk and egg then add to the bowl of flour. Whisk to remove lumps then add the mustard and a handful of cheese. Stir the ingredients together. Heat oil or butter in a medium-sized frying pan. Add a ladle of batter to the pan, swirl around and cook on one side. Before turning your pancake, drop a handful of cooked pasta onto the uncooked batter then cover with a handful of cheese. Now turn your pancake so the batter cooks and the cheese crisps up. Serve hot.

Norwegian pancakes

Ingredients

3 large eggs
1 cup all-purpose flour
1/2 teaspoon salt
1 1/2 cups milk
2 Tablespoons melted butter
Butter to fry the pancakes
Lingonberry sauce

Directions

In large bowl, beat eggs well. Whisk in flour and salt and then add in melted butter. Gradually whisk in milk until the batter is smooth. In a hot, non-stick skillet, fry ¼ of a cup of batter at a time with a little bit of butter. Flip when the top appears to be set. Roll the pancakes up and add lingonberry sauce.

Oatmeal, cottage cheese and banana pancakes

Ingredients

1/2 cup gluten-free old-fashioned rolled oats
1/2 medium banana
1/2 teaspoon vanilla extract
1 teaspoon baking powder
1/2 teaspoon cinnamon
2 large egg whites (or 1 egg)
1/4 cup fat free (or low-fat) cottage cheese
1-2 tablespoons unsweetened vanilla almond milk
Fresh berries or chocolate chips

Directions

Place all ingredients into a blender and blend until smooth. Lightly coat a large non-stick skillet or griddle with butter or cooking spray and heat over medium low heat. Place the batter by ¼ cup onto the hot skillet. Add the chocolate chips or berries. When bubbles start to appear flip the pancake over and cook for another 30 seconds or so. Wipe skillet clean and repeat with the rest of the mixture.

Oatmeal pancakes

Ingredients

2 cups ground oats
¼ cup 100% whole wheat flour
¾ cup non-fat Greek yogurt
1 small onion chopped
1 small tomato chopped
1½ cups water
1 tsp cooking oil to grease the pan
½ tsp baking soda
salt and pepper-according to taste
2 tablespoons Greek yogurt for garnish
5-6 grape tomatoes for garnish

Instructions

Mix ground oats and flour in a bowl. Add yogurt, water and remaining ingredients and mix well. Heat the pan and grease it lightly. Spread a small amount of batter using spoon. Cook the batter on medium heat until little bubbles appear and then flip over. Cook until both side are golden and serve warm.

Okonomiyaki (Savory Cabbage Pancake)

Ingredients

1 cup all-purpose flour
1 cup Dashi (fish broth)
1 egg
3-4 tablespoons Nagaimo (long yam), grated
1/4 teaspoon salt
1/4 teaspoon soy sauce
1/4 cabbage (about 12oz), chopped fine
3-4 green onions, chopped fine
2-3 tablespoons pickled red ginger (Benishouga, not sushi ginger), chopped fine
1 tablespoon oil
6 pieces thinly sliced pork belly
Okonomiyaki sauce or Tonkatsu sauce
Mayonnaise
Dried bonito flakes
Dried green seaweed

Directions

In a big bowl, whisk flour and Dashi (fish broth) together until smooth. Stir egg and yam to flour mixture. Season it with salt and soy sauce. Add cabbage, onions, and ginger to the batter and mix. Heat oil in a skillet, pour half of the pancake batter into an 8-inch circle, and out three pieces of pork slices on top. Fry at medium heat until the bottom becomes golden brown. Flip to fry the other side until the pork becomes crispy. Flip one more time, pork side up, and spread Okonomiyaki sauce and mayo on the pancake. Sprinkle dried green seaweed, then dried bonito flakes over the pancake. Serve hot.

Orange pancakes

Ingredients

2 large eggs
1-2 cup buttermilk
2 tablespoons melted butter
1/2 cup heavy cream
1/4 cup fresh squeezed orange juice
1 teaspoon orange zest
1/2 teaspoon salt
2 tablespoons brown sugar
1 tablespoon sugar
1 ½ teaspoons baking soda
½ teaspoon baking powder
½ teaspoon vanilla extract
2-3 cups all-purpose flour

Directions

Combine the eggs, buttermilk, butter, heavy cream, orange juice and zest in a medium bowl. Whisk until mixed. Add the remaining ingredients in the order listed. Add the flour until desired thickness is achieved. Whisk all ingredients until just mixed. Pour ¼ of a cup of batter for each pancake on skillet on a medium heat. Cook each side until golden and serve hot.

Peanut butter pancakes

Ingredients

2 cups all-purpose flour
2 tablespoons sugar
1 tablespoon baking powder
¼ teaspoon salt
2 eggs, lightly beaten
¾ cup creamy peanut butter
2 cups milk
1/3 cup peanuts, finely chopped

Directions

In a large mixing bowl combine flour and other dry ingredients. In a medium bowl whisk together eggs and peanut butter until combined. Gradually stir in milk. Add peanut butter mixture to flour mixture. Stir just until combined but still slightly lumpy. Gently stir in peanuts. Batter will be thin but will thicken slightly after standing a few minutes. Heat a lightly greased griddle or heavy skillet over medium heat. For each pancake, pour about ¼ cup batter onto griddle. Cook over medium heat until pancakes are golden brown. Turn when the tops start to bubble and serve hot.

Pecan pancakes

Ingredients

1 cup all-purpose flour
1/3 cup finely chopped pecans or walnuts, toasted
1 teaspoon granulated sugar
1 teaspoon light brown sugar
½ teaspoon baking powder
½ teaspoon ground cinnamon
¼ teaspoon baking soda
1/8 teaspoon salt
1 cup non-fat buttermilk
2 tablespoons vegetable oil
1 large egg

Directions

Stir together first 8 ingredients until well combined. Whisk together buttermilk, oil, and egg in a bowl; add to flour mixture, stirring just until dry ingredients are moistened. Pour about 1/4 cup batter for each pancake onto a hot, lightly greased griddle or large skillet. Cook pancakes until the tops are covered with bubbles. Turn and cook the other side until golden brown. Serve immediately.

Pesto pancake

Ingredients

2oz all-purpose
1 large egg
2 fluid ounces milk
Salt and white pepper
Butter for cooking
20 ounces toasted pine nuts and almonds mixed
1 small clove of garlic minced
3½ ounces ricotta cheese
Zest and juice half a lemon
20 basil leaves

Directions

Sift the flour into a bowl and break the egg into the centre. Whisk the egg into the flour and then add the milk a little at a time as you whisk. Season with the salt and white pepper. Toast the pine nuts and almonds in a dry pan until they are golden and release their scent. Combine ¾ of the nuts in food processor with the garlic, lemon zest and juice. Add most of the basil leaves. Stir in the ricotta until blended. Heat half of the butter in a pan and pour in half of the batter. Spread around the pan and let it cook until golden. Flip the pancake and spread on half of your pesto mixture. Fold the pancake and place on to a plate. Repeat with the remaining mixture. Add on the remaining nuts and basil leaves.

Potato Pancakes

Ingredients

1 (20-ounce) package refrigerated hash brown potatoes or mashed potato
¼ cup freshly grated Parmesan cheese
2 tablespoons all-purpose flour
2 cloves garlic, minced
2 large eggs, beaten
3 green onions, thinly sliced
¼ teaspoon cayenne pepper
Salt and freshly ground black pepper, to taste
2 tablespoons olive oil

Directions

In a bowl, mix together the potatoes, Parmesan, flour, garlic, eggs, green onions and cayenne pepper. Add salt and pepper, to taste. Heat olive oil in a large skillet over medium high heat. Scoop tablespoons of batter for each pancake and flatten them out with a spatula. Cook until bubbles appear and flip them over. Cook on the other side until golden brown and serve hot.

Pumpkin with butter pecan pancakes

Ingredients

2-1/2 cup all-purpose flour
1/3 cup sugar
4 teaspoons baking powder
1-1/2 teaspoon cinnamon
1 teaspoon ginger
1 teaspoon salt
1/4 teaspoon nutmeg
Pinch of ground cloves
2 cups milk
3/4 cup pumpkin puree, fresh or canned
4 tablespoons melted butter
2 eggs

Directions

Combine the flour, sugar, baking powder, cinnamon, ginger, salt, nutmeg, and cloves in a large bowl. In a separate bowl, whisk together the milk, pumpkin puree, melted butter, and eggs. Gradually pour the wet ingredients into the dry ingredients, whisking until well blended. Melt a little butter in a skillet over medium heat. Pour about 1/3 cup batter for each pancake. Cook pancakes until golden brown on each side.

Butter pecan syrup

1/2 cup pecans, chopped
1-1/2 cups real maple syrup
4 tablespoons butter
1 teaspoon vanilla extract
Pinch of salt

Melt 1 tablespoon of the butter in a saucepan, over medium heat. Add the chopped pecans. Cook for about 3 minutes, until fragrant. Add the maple syrup, butter, and vanilla extract. Continue to heat over medium heat until the butter has melted and blended with the syrup. Season with a pinch of salt. Serve hot.

Quinoa pancakes

Ingredients

1 1/2 cups water
¾ cup quinoa, rinsed
2 garlic cloves, minced
¼ teaspoon salt
2 large egg whites
1/2 cup grated Parmesan cheese
½ teaspoon dried basil
1/4 teaspoon freshly ground pepper
4 teaspoons extra-virgin olive oil
6 cups baby spinach leaves
1 cup salsa, optional

Directions

In a saucepan, heat water to boiling. Add quinoa, garlic and salt. Simmer, while covered, for about 10 minutes. Uncover the saucepan and cook 2 minutes longer until dry. Transfer to large bowl to cool. Preheat the oven to 350°. Stir egg whites, Parmesan, basil, and pepper into quinoa. In a non-stick skillet, heat 2 teaspoons of oil over medium heat. Using ¼ -cup measure, make 4 quinoa pancakes and flatten them out with a spatula. Cook until golden brown on either side and remove to a baking sheet. Repeat with remaining oil and quinoa. Bake pancakes for 5 minutes until heated through. Serve on spinach, with the optional salsa.

Raspberry oatmeal pancakes

Ingredients

1 1/2 cups all-purpose flour
3/4 cup old fashioned oats, uncooked
2 1/2 teaspoons baking powder
1 Tablespoon sugar
1/4 teaspoon salt
1 1/2 cups whole or non-fat milk
1 large egg
2 Tablespoons unsalted butter, melted
1 cup raspberries, smashed
Maple syrup, for serving

Directions

In a medium bowl, whisk together the flour, oats, baking powder, sugar and salt. In a separate medium bowl, whisk together the milk, egg and melted butter. Add the wet ingredients to the dry ingredients and stir just until combined. Fold in the smashed raspberries. Place a non-stick pan or griddle over medium-low heat. Drop about ¼ cup of the batter onto the hot pan. Once bubbles form, flip the pancakes once and continue cooking 1 to 2 more minutes until the pancakes are cooked throughout. Serve the pancakes with maple syrup and extra raspberries.

Red velvet cheesecake pancakes

Ingredients

1 cup flour
3 teaspoons baking powder
½ teaspoon salt
3 tablespoons sugar
1 tablespoons cocoa powder
2 tablespoons butter, melted
1 egg, beaten
¾ cup buttermilk
1½ teaspoons vanilla
1 teaspoon red food coloring
4 ounces cream cheese
For the icing
1.5 cups powdered sugar
2 ounces cream cheese
Cream, or half and half, or milk
¼ teaspoon vanilla

Directions

Slice cream cheese lengthwise into long thin pieces, wrap in plastic wrap, and freeze ideally overnight but a couple of hours is fine. Preheat a large pan or non-stick skillet to medium heat. In a large bowl add flour, baking powder, salt, sugar, cocoa powder and whisk together until combined. In another bowl add the beaten egg, buttermilk, vanilla, red food coloring and mix until blended.

Make a well in the middle of the dry ingredients and pour in the wet ingredients. Mix until all ingredients are combined. Remove cream cheese from freezer and cut into ½ inch pieces. Stir cream cheese pieces into pancake batter. Pour ¼ cup batter onto prepared pan or skillet. Cook until top begins to bubble. Flip and cook until golden brown. Remove to eat immediately or keep warm in the over.

Whisk all icing ingredients together in a medium sauce pan and heat over low heat. Drizzle over pancakes.

Ricotta and blueberries pancakes

Ingredients

1 cup all-purpose flour
¼ cup sugar
1 teaspoon baking powder
¼ teaspoon salt
2 cups water
1/3 cup sugar
1/3 cup honey
1 1/2 teaspoons vanilla extract
1 cup ricotta cheese
2/3 cup blueberries
Melted butter

Directions

Whisk the flour, sugar, baking powder and salt in a medium bowl for the pancake mix and put aside. Stir 1/3 cup of water and sugar in a small saucepan over medium heat until the sugar dissolves. Stir in the honey. Set aside. Stir the remaining 1 and 2/3 cups of water and vanilla in a large bowl. Add the pancake mix and stir just until moistened but still lumpy. Stir in the ricotta into the pancake mixture, then stir gently to add in the ricotta but maintain a lumpy batter. Fold in the blueberries. Heat a griddle over medium heat and cover with melted butter. Put about ¼ cup of batter onto the griddle for each pancake. Cook until bubbles appear on one side and then turn over for about a minute. Serve with the honey syrup.

Sausage and cheese pancake

Batter

2 eggs
2 cups of all-purpose flour
1 cup of skim milk, more if needed
1/4 cup Buttermilk
1/2 teaspoon salt
1 tsp. Baking powder
Pinch of baking soda
Pinch of sugar

Filling

Cream cheese-room temperature
Any type of grated cheese
Sausage /baked in the oven

Directions

Mix eggs with salt, baking powder, baking soda and sugar. Add flour and mix. Add buttermilk and milk and whisk together until you have a smooth and thick batter. Preheat your round pan or skillet with a drop of oil. With a half full ladle put the batter in the hot pan. It will be about a third of a cup – just a little bigger than normal. When it is golden brown turn it over and let it cook for about 30 seconds more.

Take the pancake out, spread cream cheese, put about a handful of cheese and one or two baked sausages depending how big your pancake is. Roll it and then cut into thick segments. The cheese inside will quickly melt for a delicious and hearty treat. Serve with some fresh vegetables on the side.

Smoked salmon and lemon chive cream pancakes

Ingredients

1/4 cup light sour cream
2 tablespoons chopped fresh chives
1 teaspoon grated fresh lemon rind
2.25 ounces all-purpose flour (about 1/2 cup)
1/2 cup yellow cornmeal
1 teaspoon sugar
1/4 teaspoon baking soda
1/4 teaspoon kosher salt
1/8 teaspoon ground red pepper
1 1/4 cups corn kernels
2/3 cup low-fat buttermilk
3 tablespoons butter, melted
1 large egg
12 thin slices cold-smoked salmon (about 6 ounces)

Directions

Combine first the sour cream, chives and lemon rind in a small bowl and chill in the fridge. Combine flour, cornmeal, sugar, baking soda, salt and pepper in a medium bowl. Add 1 cup corn kernels, buttermilk, butter, and egg into a blender and process until coarsely pureed. Add pureed corn mixture to flour mixture, stirring until combined. Add in the remaining 1/4 cup corn.

Pour about ¼ cup of batter for each pancake onto a hot non-stick griddle and spread gently with a spatula. Cook until bubbles start to appear and turn pancakes over. Cook until golden brown. Top the pancake with a single slice of salmon and one teaspoon lemon-chive cream.

Sourdough pancakes

Ingredients

¾ cup sourdough starter
1 egg, beaten
2 tablespoons water
2 teaspoons vegetable oil
1/3 cup non-fat dry milk powder
¾ teaspoon salt
1 teaspoon baking soda
1 ½ tablespoons white sugar

Directions

In a large bowl, combine the sourdough starter, egg, water, and oil.
In a separate bowl, combine the non-fat dry milk, salt, baking soda,
and sugar. Stir to blend dry ingredients. Add to sourdough starter
and mix until batter is smooth. Bake on a greased griddle at about
350F until golden brown on the bottom. Flip and bake on opposite
side.

Spinach pancakes

Ingredients

2 cups chopped spinach (or any other very finely chopped vegetable)
½ cup flour
1 teaspoon salt
2 large eggs
2 teaspoons dried basil
Pepper, to taste
½ teaspoon garlic powder
Butter or canola oil (for frying)

Directions

Chop the vegetables and place in a large bowl. Add the rest of the ingredients, with the flour going in last. Mix everything together. Heat oil in a skillet over medium heat. Add a ¼ of a cup into the pan for each pancake. Cook each side until golden brown. Remove and serve hot.

Strawberry pancakes

Ingredients

1 1/4 cups all-purpose flour
2 tablespoons granulated sugar
2 teaspoons baking powder
1/2 teaspoon salt
1 large egg
1 cup milk
½ teaspoon pure vanilla extract
1 tablespoon unsalted butter, melted, plus more for serving
2 cups sliced strawberries
Pure maple syrup, for serving

Directions

In a medium bowl, whisk together the flour, sugar, baking powder and salt. In a small bowl, whisk together the egg, milk and vanilla. Preheat a non-stick griddle over medium heat. Whisk the wet ingredients into the dry. Stir in the melted butter. Fold in the strawberries. Spoon the batter onto the griddle ¼ cup at a time. Cook the pancakes until they start to bubble. Flip them and cook until golden brown on the other side. Serve with butter and maple syrup.

Super-indulgent triple chocolate pancakes

Ingredients

2 large eggs
1 cup milk
3 tablespoons cooking oil
1-1/2 cups all-purpose flour
1/3 cup sugar
1 tablespoon baking powder
3 tablespoons cocoa powder
1/2 teaspoon salt
1/2 cup chocolate chips
Cooking oil, butter or margarine
Chocolate sauce or hot fudge sauce

Directions

In a medium bowl, whisk eggs until blended. Add milk and oil; whisk to combine. In a small bowl, stir together flour, sugar, baking powder, cocoa and salt until blended. Stir in chocolate chips. Add dry ingredients to liquid ingredients and then whisk until combined. Heat frying pan or griddle over medium heat (adding a small amount of oil to grease surface if using a non-stick pan). Drop about ¼ cup of pancake batter per pancake onto the griddle.

When the bubbles appear on the top flip the pancakes and cook second side until golden brown. This will take about a minute. Remove pancakes and either serve straightaway or keep warm in the oven. Serve with chocolate or hot fudge sauce.

Sweet potato pancakes

Ingredients

1 1/4 cups roasted, mashed sweet potatoes
½ cup sour cream
¾ cup milk
1 large egg
1 ½ tablespoons maple syrup, plus more for serving
4 tablespoon butter, divided
1 cup all-purpose flour
¾ teaspoon baking powder
¼ teaspoon baking soda
¼ teaspoon kosher salt
Pinch nutmeg
Pinch cinnamon

Directions

Combine sweet potatoes, sour cream, milk, egg, and maple syrup in a medium bowl. Melt 2 tablespoons butter in the microwave or in a small saucepan and add to mixture. Whisk until homogenous. Combine flour, baking powder, baking soda, kosher salt, nutmeg, and cinnamon in a large bowl and whisk to combine. Add wet ingredients to dry and whisk until just combined. Melt 1 tablespoon remaining butter in a large skillet over medium heat and swirl around. Add four 1/4-cup batches of batter, using a spatula to smooth them. Cook, until bubbles show on the first side. Flip and cook until browned on second side. Transfer to a plate set in a warm oven and repeat until all pancakes are cooked. Serve hot!

Zucchini Zinger Pancakes

Ingredients

2 shredded zucchini
1 teaspoon salt
2 large eggs, lightly beaten
3 cups of whole-wheat flour
4 cups crumbled feta cheese
4 scallions, greens and whites, chopped
1 tablespoon of olive or vegetable oil

Directions

Put the shredded zucchini in the colander and sprinkle with the salt. Set the colander in the bowl. Using your hand, press down on the zucchini so that as much liquid as possible drains out into the bowl. Stir the zucchini and repeat. Throw away the liquid. Put the zucchini in the bowl and add the eggs, flour, cheese, and scallions. Mix all everything together. Put the skillet on the stove and turn the heat to medium. When the skillet has warmed up add the oil. Using the tablespoon, scoop the mixture from the bowl and spread it into a circle (roughly 2-inch diameter) on the skillet.

Cook until the bottoms are deeply golden then turn the pancakes over and cook for four minutes. Repeat with the remaining mixture.

45512539R00033